MW01378891

Erin Elizabeth Smith

Amy—
Go Illini? Or
go Illini who Rock!
♡

Copyright © 2011 by Erin Elizabeth Smith

Cover image by Rhonda Lott

Published by Gold Wake Press
& J. Michael Wahlgren

ISBN 10: 0-9826309-8-0
ISBN 13: 978-0-9826309-8-3

No part of this book may be reproduced
except in brief quotations and in reviews
without permission from the publisher.

The Naming of Strays,
Erin Elizabeth Smith

Boston, MA

The Naming of Strays

Acknowledgements

Many thanks to the following journals where poems in this collection originally appeared:

blossombones: Emer and I Discuss Wait
Boxcar Poetry Review: Penelope
Cider Press Review: February
Gulf Stream: The Myth of Independence
Harpur Palate: Willing
Limestone: A Journal of Art and Literature: Drinking Poem
The Lindenwood Review: Index of the Midwest, The Way the Cold Attaches
New Delta Review: Spring Again in Hattiesburg
NOO Poetry: When I Think of Sorrow I Think of Sparrows
Pacific Review: Aromatics, How to Fall in Love
Product: Cityscapes, Gravity of Light
Rougarou: On Asking My Lover Not to Move to London
Salamander: Love Poem
Silk Road: Driving in Mississippi Next to Two Men I've Slept With
Specs: At the New York State Museum
Sunsets and Silencers: Binghamton, On Being Erroneously Called a New Yorker Again
Trailer Park Quarterly: Ghost Limb, Love in Mississippi
Water ~ Stone Review: Sherbet
Wicked Alice: A Box of Paperclips, Drawing What I Hear
Yalobusha Review: It's Spring and Everyone's Writing Love, Lovebugs

"Closet Space" first appeared in *Eating Her Wedding Dress: A Collection of Clothing Poems* (Ragged Sky Press), and "Fidelity" first appeared in *The Southern Poetry Anthology: Mississippi* (Texas Review Press). "Drawing What I Hear" also appeared in *narrative (dis)continuities: prose experiments by younger american writers* (VOX Press).

for The Clubhouse

"Forget about the beds of middle America,
you don't need the fat of the man."
-Erin McKeown

Table of Contents

I.

Sweet	15
Aromatics	16
Elemental	17
Drawing What I Hear	18
Sherbet	19
When I Think of Sorrow I Think of Sparrows	20
Willing	21
Index of the Midwest	22
Transformation	23
Overpass	24
How to Fall in Love	25

II.

The Way the Cold Attaches	29
February	30
Winter	31
Charity	32
Ghost Limb	33
My fear is simple, heart-faced	34
Penelope's Kitchen	35
On Asking My Lover Not to Move to London	36
The Patience of Emer	37
Emer and I Discuss Wait	39
Flammable	40
Fidelity	41

III.

The Myth of Independence	45
Love in Mississippi	47
Binghamton	48
At the New York State Museum	50
On Being Erroneously Called a New Yorker Again	51
Secret Love Song	52
Penelope	53
A Box of Paperclips	55
Drinking Poem	56
Still Life With Cook After One-Night Stand	58
Driving in Mississippi Next to Two Men I've Slept With	59
Lovebugs	60

IV.

The Naming of Strays	63
Swiftness to Ash	64
Theories of the Earth	65
On Learning to Be Okay	66
Closet Space	67
Gravity of Light	68
It's Spring and Everyone's Writing Love	69
Love Poem	70
Cityscapes	71
Snow in Mississippi	72
All Things Rare	73
Spring Again in Hattiesburg	74

I.

stray (v.) to wander from the direct way, deviate.

Sweet

Sweet is the first taste. The wet scrawl
of it in the ridges of suckling
mouths. Do not discount it.
The cardamom pop in the peaches,
Michigan cherries bitten
to the stem. So quick
to forget these for the salamander
lighting of sugar and cream,
ceremony in the slow bowing
of a head. This is what comes
later. First the jam-sweet breakfast
and a television, the long couch
strewn with blankets and cleaved books.

Sweet in the swift
lips on a shoulder. Hands grasping
across a front seat. Or red
crocuses, the dim-lighting lamp
by the bedside and its click.
The dimple of bodies
that have been recycled. How we hold
our hand to the place long
marked in our mattress,
the shape of sweet so often
turned, so fluffed and feathered
that we too lose its form.

Aromatics

On his countertop
in a pair of black heels,
I waited for him
to say we were through,
while we made a soup
of portobello, lentils,
kale. I stirred
while the broth boiled
into steam, its deep
tomato red thawing
the house. He chopped
garlic into fine squares.
In bed I licked its scent
from his skin.

Months later, he calls
to give back my pan.
We meet in the city,
that meal a ghost story –
the dead who rose
in supermarkets
to buy rosemary and wine.
I stand in the street,
the black weight
in my hand and think
about the smoky paprika,
Hungarian sausage,
one yellow onion gone
translucent in the base –
as the fever of the city's ovens
rises up in that single-bladed cold.

Elemental

The child burns

like the scaled backs
of summer skinks,
the poker-hot feel
of ribs through skin.

Or rather we think she does,
beneath the cycling smoke
on Midwestern horizons.
We imagine the kettle sigh

in a red window,
a voice in some neighbor's
farmhouse turned
an ibisco of flame.

Do we save her?
Secure our lungs
in their flesh sacks
and pull the pinafored girl

to our hot, freckled cheek.
Does she belong to us?
Can she speak anymore?
Put her on that island

that's too green to burn.
Hold her so still
that the ember
draws from the limbs.

Drawing What I Hear

In the coffee shop, the last time I see him, I hear him move from me. A friend says *I don't know what he'll do. I don't like him anymore.* She is talking about her husband. There is a swallow in my throat. Water drips into a pot. Steam. My body is shrill, the way the lids lower and brush to him. His hat, his shirt, they make no noise, but they did when he threw them on his bed, always unmade, always cold and expectant. Though some nights last winter we made it warm and I heard him say my name. And him saying, *Wait. No.* Then the turning of my body in his hands. The sounds of sheets bunched at the heels. The night he told me about the ex who held him like me. I hear his sink drip in the bathroom and do not rise to stop it. Dishes collapse in the sink. The *click-click-click* of a pilot light and the opening conversation of flame. The near silent way his hand covered mine at the bar the night I met him. The night he said *Come in.* And I did. And here today, my friend saying *He was never this way. Or he always was.* I say *Come here,* and her hair makes a sound across my cheek. I do not hear the closed door of his leaving, his car start up in the lot. Instead I remember fingers in his hair the last day I knew him. The way I didn't say his name when he left. The way the air didn't raise its breath to voice, but it could have been the sound of his voice. The sound of his voice saying *No* and then the brushfire in my bones, the low, long crackle.

Sherbet

In line at the store, a man
is buying sherbet and sugar cones.
His tropical neapolitan of iced fruit
in front of my basket
of red pepper, fleshy eggplant.

Tonight, alone, I'll make rice for curry,
a bottle of green paste whisked
through canned milk, heat in the nose
from backyard jalapeños. I'll roll
basil like tobacco, snipping
ends into the pot, dice greens
into parchment strips and cradle
the bowl in my lap.

This man could be buying
his plastic-bellied sweetness for children,
a woman who bathes open-doored,
loves to kiss the cool lime syrup
from him after he lips his way to the cone,

but it's only sadness I can see —
his drooped neck, the unzipped
windbreaker opened to a grey shirt,
spoons in the soft, milky fruit,
of someone alone touching
his tongue to the cold
center of impossible pink.

Willing

In my sleep I dream endlessly of birds,
      the mathematics of jazz.
      Grey-winged finches in a fan kick.

Rain shutters the morning.
      The azaleas, like children,
      climb onto anything that will hold still.

The showerhead drips,
          almost a song.
Let this, all this, be a lesson, it hums.
      The waking,
      the absence,
      the bluebird

          crushed in the polished parking lot.

When I Think of Sorrow I Think of Sparrows

When I think of sorrow I think of sparrows. And zebra finches flushing to twice their size then shrinking again to something small that disappears. I think of the rabbit that watches me from the lawn that doesn't run when I startle it walking to the laundromat in my pajamas tipsy though they say wine might be good for me. And really I still smile when I watch the squirrels chase each other along the telephone line but on a night like tonight I can't see myself alive in twenty years though I can see myself in the kitchen, in anybody's kitchen, closing my eyes, biting down on a barrel like it's a muffin like it's cake. And there are times when the shape of my hand on my thigh is almost enough. When the warm summer rain is almost enough. When the phone ringing in the other room is like a sparrow singing in the too-late morning when I'm still in bed when I'm watching the ceiling waiting for it to open to cave in. Waiting for the neighbor's dog to start barking for the fire engines blowing through the red lights for the moment when I turn and realize no one's there and that someone could be. That the bed is too big. That there are squirrels in every city and they could all be the same. Realize there will never be a time when it feels easy. Realize no matter how much I wish it the ceiling is solid and the rain has passed and I'm here and cold and walking in the street at midnight with a basket of sheets. Realize the rabbit has such large eyes and when I feint toward it, it takes off into the street. And somehow I'm surprised when its tail flashes like a lighthouse like a mirror in the sun.

Index of the Midwest

The name of a bridge
leads to the voice
of someone who I almost forgot
I slept with to a street
I got lost on to the pink slip
of tongue between a housecat's teeth.
The industrial corn stretching
into an endless factory
of gold, nights in the dark
lake water, breaking in
a front porch like a ship.
Beggar's purses
with cheddar and corn.
Shot glasses like church
windows and afternoons
smoking Camel Lights. No coming
to peace. No leaf turning
on an ancient record player.
If only there had been an escape hatch
in August's shorn fields. One that falls
forever into this flat
and desperate black.

Transformation

What precise arcs of color
in transformation. First a girl
becomes a walking stick, then
a lioness licking back

a full mane. Each flirtation
apes solidity, each thrust
hip spirals into toothpaste,
green tea in a microwave.

I need to be a thimble
on a girl's tiny right hand.
The chartreuse drip of evening.
Sliced starfruit. A dashing man.

I cannot be this lounge chair
in the spiced sun forever.

Overpass

Running this morning,
I stood above the interstate traffic,

the dulled earth color of cars
beneath. I held

my knees and breathed
through a wide mouth,

the green mileage signs to cities
unreadable in the distance.

He was not there but
I wanted to tell him

about the trucks
like long-bodied swimmers,

the steadfast pine
green and needled again

from the last storm that shucked them.
And how watching it all

alone, breath filled the muscle
and the heart was revved

and flooded with blood.

How to Fall in Love

Here is where you pack the heart – in a small dark box. A box cut for heart-shaped things. Like a case for a French horn, a crystal paperweight. It can be stored anywhere – in a cool linen closet, in the cat-eyed dark beneath your bed. You may line the box with tissue. You may spin the combination on its lock. You may look at it sadly or punch the fist-sized object with your own closed palm. But you must forget it, must not dream about its soprano in the shower, its sleepy Southern drawl.

Once it is packed and put away, go outside. The sun will set, but before it does, it will pour hotly onto your shoulders. It will sink into your neighbor's roof, and as it turns the sky a candy-colored blue, you must say aloud *It will not be like this again. It cannot.* When you do, there will be a moment when you turn back toward your house. You will see a kitchen window, a shovel leaning against your porch – and it will be transformed. Touch the doorknob. Hold it firmly in your hand until it's warm. Then turn it. Turn it slowly. You must go back in.

II.

stray (v.) to wander from the path of rectitude, to err.

The Way the Cold Attaches

There's just one more story I have
to tell you. In it, it's December
and I'm looking out a window,
the street brown with snow.
Your car is not pulling to my curb,
though with every leaf of movement
I think it might.

If only this wasn't
the story – instead, you
in a museum, looking for me,
me looking for you. Yet there
we find the other, and we know
that's not true. Is it, instead,
me getting out of your car
that last Thursday we were lovers?
When you waved, I didn't
know what you meant;
I'd written the sense
from your hands – those four
lined fingers, the pressing thumb.

I don't know how to live
here. The December trees are slight
beneath their coats, so achingly
cold. Maybe this is the story –
in the park this afternoon
the snow stretched across the grass,
ice-bright. I watched the city
simmer on the other side,
and there I was the only woman
and you were not
the only man.

February

Two days before my mother's birthday,
the daffodils nub their way through

Champaign's arctic lawn – the bellybuttons
of blonde opening as they do back home,

the yellow that signifies rest or resolve.
Like how the Southern forsythia breaks

in the blushing spring, the dandelions
with their removable heads, their roots

that suck at the planless earth.
Yet here in Mississippi the magnolia is still

hunched and green, though the hot morning
seeped through my window like chamomile

as if light could become a body,
as if this season could build from it home.

Winter

Winter is a pony-tailed redhead,
displeased with the undoing of her work.
She has laid siege to April, sucked the small buds
from the sugar maple, and now sits on my couch
flipping channels.

"What do you want me to say?" she smirks.
"All this death, it makes me feel cut and polished again.
The geese digging for their supper under my skirt.
Man, I may leave Persephone in that gutter
until she lilts and sings my name like a blue jay."

She lights a cigarette, taps the ashes on the floor.
"Listen, girl. You think a goddamn fruit basket
is gonna get me out of here? I can freeze the Mississippi,
Wall Street, the White Knoll Elementary school buses
with my fingernails." She leans forward, smiles.

"Spring is my bitch. She'll come,
but only when I tell her to."

Charity

after Rubens' "Roman Charity"

Red is the beginning,
the neckline lapsing
into the cupped white
breast she holds to him
like a spoon. In his eyes
is the feasting
of mealworms, a gnashing
feral hunger. For me it is the same,
my legs pocked by brick, the quick
wildflower of hands
eclipsing a knee. The wet sand
that gives to the feet.
What alms do we have
but unbuttoning,
an erection of French bread,
my blushed winter nose,
that canvas
of shoulder blade
in some man's dark,
humming room.

Ghost Limb

> *Depression is boring, I think.*
> -Anne Sexton

Happiness is boring, I think, an oasis
between sand and the close-fitting heat.
Between the shuffling din
of traffic and tail lights
that blink in a motionless draw.

I don't trust the way the days canter up,
but I'm afraid not to want it. Afraid I'll forget
where the mouth goes, where the muscle binds
tight to the bone. That I'll build a house
just to set it aflame, the cat's unearthly howl
in the quick-talking blaze.

Each day I wake in the same bed,
the ceiling white, the light in the window
like warm cream. The cat paws
at my lover who pulls me
to his chest. I know the source
of my restlessness but do not
name it,

while dawn breaks with the same
fleshy flourish as a heart
opened wide with a knife, stuck forever
on the note it began.

My fear is simple, heart-faced

after a line by Lorna Dee Cervantes

This year, again, the azaleas
will come with no trowel work,
the seeded mint hurdling up
like tiny trees. There will be blackberries

in April, and that closing shot
of Orion's winter hunt
will mark the end of my astronomy.
Once it wasn't so predictable –

one flashing gull on a boardwalk,
the slammed shot glass, the dark lip
of my stocking puckering off.
I will sit still, though, cross-legged

on a bed, reading. I will make a face
and hold it until the wet clay
sets, readies to burn brittle.
Spring no longer surprises me

with gardens or basil pastas.
Just stillness and return, some absent
promise of sonorous heat,
the drab birth of *again*.

Penelope's Kitchen

The house's walls are pocked
by nails. A linen candle tongues
another room and her landlord's
purple-petaled flowers grow despite
all attempts to smother them. Still,
her kitchen is a factory of knuckle –
white dough roughed in cornmeal,
bay leaf boats in a pot of stew.

Why does she wait for him?
Each night the solitude of spice
racks, potted rosemary, oregano,
her crossed calves like highball
glasses, a red quilt dog-eared on the bed.
Bullets of young romas
burst on their vine, while she marks
each white mug
with her veiny maps.

On Asking My Lover Not to Move to London

In maps
of the body
        this is the hand, this is the eye
cartography
is   memory
      a small, slick kayak
      the history of the sea.

  ✺

The wet blossom
arch self
      works through
      the hard
      and even distance,
the sound of morning
      like women
      slender
      in their secrets.

  ✺

You
      my meal
      my red summer tongue
come
      build me a white space,
        a song that lapses
here
      like this skin

              like this –

The Patience of Emer

> *In Celtic mythology, Emer was said to possess the*
> *six gifts of womanhood: beauty, gentle words, a sweet*
> *voice, wisdom, skill at needlework, and chastity.*

The Celtic phrase for beauty
is *skeima*, that word
that sounds the sweet
structure of certainty, the wisdom
in the slit eye of a needle,
its impossible chastity.

In the Irish loam, dogs chase
rabbits into their holes. These brutes
who do not know the charming dark, how it needles
into each den, wards
off the sunlight of defense. How wise.
If I could sleep through the sweet

nights, the sun sweating
the hair on my neck to its chaste
down, maybe I could wait – the whys
muted into the sullen beauty
of sleep and reckless dream. No words
for promise or the animal need

that reaches its fist from the needless
chest, the unanswerable sweet
tooth in a chapel of salt. And still no word
from you in that unchaste
female country. The green buttes
of Scotland where the women are wiser

needing no man, while
I must be this woman with a needle
pulled into one hole. Beautiful
as carved alabaster, a suite
of ordered music. Yet to give chase
would undo the beautiful

homecoming. To acknowledge the beauties
that belittle my absence, the wise
distance in their ribcage. No. To chase
is to act, to melt the needle
of its use. Waiting is what sweetens
and patience is both a woman's beauty

and her name. Chased, we turn into words,
trees, and brutes. Nothing so wise
as this stasis, need made ferocious and sweet.

Emer & I Discuss the Wait

> *Emer was the wife of Cu Chulaind in Celtic mythology —*
> *like Penelope she waited for her husband to return from battle*
> *to discover he'd been unfaithful.*

Is it so different? The tufted ocean impossible
to cross, the pale blue of a linked sky

that only women in flight can traverse —
bird bodies chained to their ominous drive.

Still, you and I, we cannot change
into anything but the women we are,

staring at the walls that need hangings,
the dinners cooled and sealed.

We wait while our bodies wither
like tulips each March and hope

for a crack in the ceiling, a Grecian burglary
of rain. Or simply a man that presses

his calf into ours under a table, takes
us in his room that's black as birth.

Flammable

New Orleans, 2006

Though we never set the table on fire,
we wanted to – a tundra of powdered
sugar flammable as polyester.
The next morning broke dazzling and awkward
and we had to try to go back to who
we were – acrobats of the unspoken,
the ones who could light the sweetened igloos
and blow the slim match clean above the burn.
But waking up together left us changed –
this shoulder marked in lips was no longer
my own, the skin made communal and strange
in the slim-sheeted dawn. What real danger
could there have been in restraint, bladed light
held above a simple promise of heat?

Fidelity

In the husky warmth of the Pine Belt, fidelity
is impossible. Every road leads to a home
built of sticks and straw, and the dogs
are not wolves, per se, but carnivorous as love.
Who can hold still in this place? This bed
that opens like a curtain, the morning distant as London,

that undreamable city where you live. London,
like a memory of heat that marks the skin, the fidelity
of ghosts. Last summer, we made our bed
large with how close we slept, as if home,
for a moment, was possible. As if hope or love
could salvage us from the dogged

winter that would follow. From the bony dog
that howls outside our door. From the London
fog that doesn't rise despite how much we do not love
that shadowy unknown. It's not fidelity
that keeps a garden groomed, a home
as white as writer's block. It does not make the bed

so tight that one cannot slip in, the bedsheets
cool as they can be lonesome. I hear dogs
wail into the crisp dark, their home
turned prison in the slumber of others. In London
he calls and I'm cupped inside another man, fidelity
running empty on the long, unlit interstate. I'm sorry, love,

but the body is a field of lilies, only lovely
when there is water and sun. Green flower beds
to root and bulb in. The strict fidelities
of a growing season. Are the flowers to blame for dogs
who bury shoes in their soil, the Londons
that are built where something could bloom. Come home.

There's still time to plant peach trees. Frame a house
that's built of brick, a chimney that draws. Learn to love
the held breath, the steady hand. What does London

have over this city? Here, we could live in one bed,
make wheat four scones. Let in that wet dog
and name her Patience. Must we always keep this fidelity

to distance, to London's ancient, chilly homes?
In paintings, fidelity is not a flower or love
or one-manned bed, but a pale and whimpering dog.

III.

stray (v.) to wander free from control, to roam about

The Myth of Independence

I.

In my story, there is always an accident —
a vicious windmill, three imaginary deer,
my palms pressed on his hips like butterflies.

It will happen. A teacup dropped in a diner.
Him, sunglassed and stupid from the heat,
turning in his booth.

II.

I dreamt of him last night,
stubborn as Southern dogwood
that spends the spring taunting bloom.

Yet something in me wanted to wake
and find him there, braiding my hair,
looking to the sun as it raises its hand.

III.

What I want —
someone who appreciates the mortality of the South,
how New Orleans keeps its dead above water.

Someone with wide palms
who will wonder at the flatness
of our roads, the shape of my missing accent.

IV.

When he says to come with him, what is he asking?
For me to chase him across the map like a river?
To become the ink for his pen?

To be that girl, who gave
her body as a gift,
he says I could be so lovely then.

Love in Mississippi

is always a metaphor. Sheep
grazing on the heath,
the grinding of vegetables
into a cool green soup.
Corridors of halogen
mark the straight routes
home, the turns we miss
or accidentally take.
Like the boxed pansies
or the woman who owns
a badger and walks it
in the park. Rather no,
that was love in New York
where the rivers erected
themselves in the patchwork spring
and the windows were so small
even I could not slip through.

Binghamton

*On April 6, 2009, a gunman opened fire on a center
where immigrants were taking a citizenship exam
in downtown Binghamton, killing thirteen.*

It's not hard to remember
her through the television
snapshots – the congressional
church on Main looking out
along the strip of chicken
joints and the red brick high school.
Everything needing
a good scrub from the salty
winters, industrial closings,
her sad desire to be reborn.

A thousand miles away,
and everyone's saying her name
like I never left, like she is sitting
on my porch again,
fingering the mimosa she killed
in its clay pot. I can almost touch her
even here, in this Southern city,
where the bushes turn twenty
shades of pink in February
and the deafening grey
of the rainy season is but a bluster
of winter and then the pirouetting spring.

It's as blue today in Mississippi
as it was that September in New York
when the great cats of those buildings
skinned themselves to ash.
I stared out my window that day too,
looking at her in the backyard,
the thistle crinkling violet on the green.
A stray cat rolled and rolled in my garden,
turned up its newly brown body
and hopped the fence.

That's most of what I remember of that day,
and I look at my own cats,
chasing each other in and out
of my car's tires and wonder if this
is how I'll see her now—
the vested police with their long guns,
a blockade of lights and firearms.
My one loved city reduced
to headlines, her proximity
from New York. And me so useless
and distant, wanting nothing
but a home to cradle her in.

At the New York State Museum

I obsess about the wired flight
of starlings, how despite
their nature, they do not snap
at the songbirds in this mobile,
nor call – car sirens and snags
of dialogue in the throat.
Their freckled chest heaveless
and the marbles of their eyes
black as punctuation.

Does every state have birds strung
to a ceiling? In my hometown,
these same histories – the colonial
scepter in the statehouse lit up
behind glass, the limed dome
before its new pennyness.
At our museum, a barricade
of palmettos, cannonballs like wet
footprints, dioramas of wrens
and red hawks straining to break
their bent tethers, windows
sealed to their escape.

On Being Erroneously Called a New Yorker Again

It's not that I don't want
your palate of hill, roughed up
autumn color. I would take it all —
the stones in the dried Susquehanna,
the candy sunsets and all slow turns
on the dark drive to Ithaca.

I would take the closed summer rinks,
the children clung
on the necks of carousel mares.
Stretches of surprising cows
and corn and the barns
long sunk into themselves.
Take the imploding
shoe factory, the starving doors
of IBM, the remains of the Art
Theater, its five years of ash.

I'd take the terrible pink
of that retirement home
and scrape it to its bergamot beginnings.
Wash the arena windows
until they shone like dimes,
dress all the bandages
on the heels of you, my city, and lullaby
the mounded snow to spring.

But I inherited another city —
dimpled palmetto forts, the dignity
of Southern dead, songs about cars,
cornbread and cast iron. Where I'm from,
we do not believe in New York,
but still, I'm Wendy,
sometimes, in her bed,
staring into the sad black
of a story that is no longer mine.

Secret Love Song

Six months ago, I had a dream everything was white –
    the walls, the pillows, my body slim and sunless on the sheets.
        And you were there, not the man I fell to sleep with,

hands mapping my body, face lit like a chandelier.
    There is something I needed to tell you.
        Not this dream, though when I woke,

my chest felt like the walls of something lived in.
    No, it was that we should have known, that night in November,
        when the wind was bitter and smelled of snow.

When we broke to find our cars in the cold, waving
    as if our hands were the flags of two nations,
        small and close enough to be one.

Penelope

First, I planted hyacinth in the courtyard,
pruning the wayward petals, which wilted
at my over-attendance, my heavy watering can.

Next, I made robes for your father, brushing the velvet
'til it was colt-soft and bright. Polished the buttons,
weaved gold into his yellow cords.

In the fifteenth year, I took to oils, turning the strokes
of my tedium into your distant ship. I painted you
a thousand ways – falling from the mast, the prow,

from the ocean into the even ebb of Styx.
Then my doorbell took to sounding.
I was forced to replace the welcome mat

with "Beware of Dog." But men persisted,
revived my gardens, dry-cleaned the robes,
auctioned my mid-day sketches for kingdoms.

I took to tapestry only then to dissuade
their ardent verse, their gracious doors and coats.
This I loved though – the goldfish

of my hands slipping the weave. Creating
a cape of scenery, a story of thread.
I was patient with my unraveling, promising

once I finished this, my centerpiece, my heart
of cotton, I would take another from the sea –
a strange jellyfish, a bright and foreign conch.

So when you arrived with your exultation
of flag, I was the first to welcome you,
with a limp albatross, two arms at the ledge.

But now that you're back, eating with your fingers,
grabbing my thighs in sleep, while another
woman churns in your skin,

I leave the waiting for the tired
sun, paper our house with tapestry,
finish everything I begin.

A Box of Paperclips

In some ways it's simple. Here
is the weight of a hand, a box
of paperclips laid on a chest. The wet
heat of Mississippi, a longing
of the bones to be free
of the skin, the way they lean
from the body
into the frenetic air.

Or the hollowed skull
of an acorn squash. A postcard
on a refrigerator door.
The haloes of street lamps
and that unformed object
at the end of the trail.

Love, what does this turn
us into? What does distance do
except open like a split geode
to reveal itself – blue and cracked
and impossibly hard.

Drinking Poem

I was probably drunk.
It's amazing more poems don't begin
this way – the shot glass
O of my mouth against his
on the loveseat. My bones so small,
like he was a slat wood
raft, a causeway through
the dirty Pontchartrain.

The day before my boyfriend came
home from London
I woke up with my pants
inside-out, a slit-eyed
memory of myself in someone's
bathroom, fumbling
with my tongued pockets.
And the day after he said
he would leave again,
I closed the bar
with another man, who cupped
my knee in his white horse
of a car and sucked
the air from between
our drowned bodies.

There's no forgiveness
in empty bottles, the silent
teeth of blackouts on bourbon
and cheap shiraz, but today
I found my landlord's pinwheel flowers
had become ten thousand blackberries
licking up my chain-link fence.
And my bell peppers have popped
from their starry beginnings
into the hardened fetus of fruit.

I wonder sometimes
if patience turns us hard
like the hulled seeds of pumpkins
left to heat. Wait translated
into nothing more
than the brief pyrotechnics
of skin, the sure pop
of a button through its hole.
That long burn of a cigarette
outside my favorite dive.

Still Life with Cook after One-Night Stand

An uncooked bird needs
brining, its pale rubber body

sink-warm. There are cranberries
to bleed. Lettuce to crack and clean.

Garlic cloves to brown into sweetness
and shallots peeled to the tooth.

There are peppers she must stuff
then yeast to warm into rolls. A pound

of pecans. A bottle of Viognier. The stirring
of wild mushrooms, marjoram, vine-ripe

tomato. While he sleeps, she stares
at his watermarked ceiling, consumed

with timing, temperature, and the morning
birds with their impatient, ugly song.

Driving Next to Two Men I've Slept With

Outside Pascagoula, there's a store we pass
advertising liquor and knives. In the bayou, the trees
don't speak, but deal in secrets

and human combustion. March, already –
the azaleas stain the graying brick houses,
while forsythia sinks into its long wait.

We are three in this car but were once two –
and two again. We try to believe nothing
before this highway existed, these bodies that sheen

like blades. And no one notices as we move
soundlessly across the red ground,
past chronicles of scrub pine and parked cars,

names sighed in other men's beds. If only
it were possible to be only a woman
in the backseat slowly drawing water to her mouth.

Lovebugs

Honeymoon flies, telephone bugs,
a life of endless in-flight copulation.
They swarm the humidity from the Gulf
to the Carolinas. Not a true bug
in the order *Hemiptera*, but a fly
that lifts from grassy lands, siphons
the nectar of magnolia, oleander. They bang
into banisters, off the flushed cheeks of men
waiting for buses, a girl's open-mouthed laughter.
The slow drift of insects like campfire ash,
the splashed bodies Pollocked
on each bumper, love turned
beast and blood in the streets.

IV.

stray (n.) An animal that has strayed or wandered away from its flock, home, or owner.

The Naming of Strays

You never know what the preamble will look like —
wrought-iron tables, pasted napkins
on the butts of steins, my elbow
and his pitched in conversation.

Later, the wet shawl of night
on my spotted shoulders, I marvel
at how he does not touch me.
Two years of floundering in unmade beds —
bar rat's rooms with their armies of tossed laundry,
abandoned dryer sheets — and I am fearful
of absence, the bare feeling of my legs
slipping from the dress.

But this night is different. The playground
across the street with its stilled swings, my cat
clipping between his legs, the sweetness
in how this man touches its back, the arching
acceptance, a language it alone understands.

For weeks, this black tom roamed my parking lot,
the bottom half of lizards zipped in its teeth.
Without a name, it was homeless —
no backdoor where it could smuggle
squirrels, no stretch of shoulders
to paw on afternoon beds.

Maybe love is simply the naming of strays.
And any name will do. Each comes
equally from the lips to make him
gallop towards us
through the yard
and home.

Swiftness to Ash

They are burning pizza boxes in the backyard.
The woman drenches wood with gasoline,
throws in hedge clippings, a pyre
of rhododendron, butterfly bush,
while the man tosses beer boxes onto the blaze.
Each blue opening melts to black,
the abrupt burst of flame and its swift retreat.
The wood holds, heat in its splintery bones,
while they marvel at the swiftness of smoke and ash.
In the dark, they sit together
on a plastic chair certain anything
they hold could smolder.

Theories of the Earth

Nothing is so old
that it can't be transformed.
The deep time that builds
then potholes the land
can be as shallow as teeth
turned dun in the mouth.
The silver-dollar
bruise on the top floor
of a thigh becomes skin again
and pale. New Mexico's
ship-shaped rock may
weather into a black quarter
horse, then a television set. It is not
the flood that makes the rock,
but the churning earth
fluffed with breath
then packed again.
And the soil can hold each
five-pound cut of coal,
the ground shrubs scared up
with titmice, and the slippery distance
between toothpick forests
and downtown boutiques.
Outside a girl rides her purple bike
beside the road, while another
changes the banks
of her backyard stream
damming it with stone after stone
from its own bed.

On Learning To Be Okay

On leaving the bus
I smile and tell the driver
Thanks. It is easy
giving this to him, taking
what he gives back.
Then I walk home
on the curbs. I do not
crush acorns
with the flat of my boot
or shoot gravel
into the neighbor's yard.
Instead I wonder why
every pencil I own
must be sharp,
every shirt ironed flat.
I do not think
about spring
or how it feels
to be loved –
nor do I think about killing
the house spider that floats
down my living room
wall. I do not want a hand
any hand
on my knee or the phone
to sing out from the still.
I do not wash
every dish I dirty
or pull tight
the sheets to dig in them
again. Instead,
at home, I make
a thick pea soup
and listen
to the radiator
as it bangs
its way to life.

Closet Space

I haven't decided what to wear,
my closet plagiarized from other lives –
the lime halter I doffed in New Orleans,
the burnt orange tube top with Zodiac broach,
ruffled zebra print, white linen
pinked in the wash. I wonder how many
floors they have slept on
while I thrashed in some bed,
or who brushed against them
in a supermarket, while I was buying quince
and white wine. I tug at the hem
of a black skirt that used to be too small,
a collared shirt I've undone
so many times, the buttons
like the long whole notes of song.
How simple it can be—
an entire life in a zipper,
the kick of a boot to the floor.

Gravity of Light

Where do we place this? Spring
with its parceling bloom, radiator
blue horizons laced with dogwood and pine.
Or winter, Illinois' clean cold buffing the sky
This is not that kind
of story. Instead wall painting,
the squealing drill, that tug and pull
of red curtains through their poles.
My hand between the flapjack pillows,
eyes inked with sleep, and the long stretch
of his back against our sheets.
This could be anywhere, he says –
New York, Illinois, the sweet
pea green of Ireland –
and sometimes it is, when morning
is barricaded at the window, his lips
huddled in the valley of my thighs.

It's Spring and Everyone's Writing Love

What easy metaphors—

The hummingbird sheen
of oil slicks, sprinklers
wetting the jalapeños
in a neighbor's side-yard,
tilted husks of hydrangea,
that impossible green
of religion.

This is not us.

Instead—

A violin of marrow. Avocados
in summer. Lime like a small ship
in stemless glass.

Love Poem

Stirling, Scotland

Rabbits gather over clover,
tails turned their unharried dun

and the loch of lidded mallards is still,
each bill tacked under the wing.

I envy this. The deliberate pause
that comes with history and age —

the way a country can rise from bed
and read to itself. The breath comes

long and steady. The skin an unhowling
spit of rain. How do I love you

like this? Here there is no distance,
no hurry to sandbag the rainless city.

To live in a space where neither must say
Come closer. Where it is just enough

for one to muster up a high hill,
while the other follows after.

Cityscapes

1. Binghamton, NY

This was the start of New York –
the hewn mountains nearly rising
with breath, winter's clean teeth
gnawing the maples. It's not
nostalgia, that word that staples
homecoming to *grief*. Rather the ear's
pillow heart, the roving home
like footfall in thick October brush.

2. Champaign, IL

Some say memory is incurable,
but the prairie state can hypnotize
anyone into thinking all that's left
is a deaf interstate, the deadlock
of the corn broken
by soy beans, skyscrapers.
No casserole dishes or dioramas
of families at the hearth.
No architectured angels in new snow.

3. Hattiesburg, MS

At night every car is the same
in this teacup city. History
a long-throated soprano or the purring
of a stray. I wasn't willed anything
but the brown South, endless stalks
of pine, unbearable crimson skin.
But the welcome sign says *Mississippi:*
It's Like Coming Home. And it is
sometimes, with its pyrotechnic
lightning, a boomerang of blackbirds
against the six o'clock sky.

Snow in Mississippi

This morning my ex called
from New York to tell me
it was snowing in Mississippi,
the first opera of white we've had
in years. My boyfriend opens
the blinds to the monosyllabic wet,
the white not unlike my years
in mulberry weather, northern
pines portly with snow, salmon
sunsets on the quilted ice.

This is not who I am now —
my cat's rough tongue
on the pane's condensation,
the distant replay of yearning
for what I might have had —
an amnesiac winter, the cutting
sun as it flips its reins over
the slender asparagus palms.

All Things Rare

With cinnamon in 'em, and all things rare!
-James Whitcomb Riley

I chalk the walls with cinnamon
to keep the ants from coming in.
What strange passages bring this spice here –
panicled flowers, ovate green popping
from the unshaved limbs
to Nero's funeral pyres,
Biblical beds perfumed in aloe
and myrrh, Solomon's bark-spiced
love. Now in a yellow rented kitchen,
that same smoky sweetness glazes
snail bread, deep red chickpea stews.
Becomes a brown band-aid
against the whip-black army lined
on the countertop. What else can quills
of sweet wood cure? Fever. History.
Spring's yellow-bodied colds.
In the groves of Sri Lanka
the toddler trees wait to be
coppiced and macerated,
transformed again into the sacrament
of bread and whetted spice.

Spring Again in Hattiesburg

Sometimes it's as simple as a house
butter-yellow against the spring.
A tree trunk ringed in monkey grass,
those sudden azaleas blinking

in the new March. This season
is here again, where last year I doffed
my bathing suit on a Slip 'n Slide
though I was twenty-seven

and sober enough to know better.
That same day, I taught you honeysuckle,
how to lick the piston sweet between the buds.
How ridiculous. The two of us

standing in our backyard, pulling
apart flowers, still in my suit,
feet muddy and caked in grass,
when we could have been

trafficking ourselves
to corporations, turning the wet
lawn into science, or populating this house
with what they call growth.

Life is not this memory, or it shouldn't be,
but there's something in the mint
that came up again this year,
cheery in the overgrown garden,

ready for tabouli, juleps, the cool
dirt of fresh herbs on the teeth.
Something in the trumpeting white
we plucked from the vine,

our bay window lit up
with balmy light, that breaks me
open like new hyacinth, that keeps

planting the same garden

despite the eaten-through tomatoes,
the late bell peppers I won't harvest
in this last year. To touch the flower
to your mouth for the first time again,

laugh at our adult nudity, the slip
of plastic on a rutted lawn,
the inevitable boxes, trunks,
and pulling away from this place,

this sun-colored house,
the things that grow while we sleep.

NOTES

The Erin McKeown quote is from her song "Fast As I Can."

The definitions of "stray" are from the 2009 *Oxford English Dictionary*.

The Anne Sexton quote in "Ghost Limb" comes from her poem "The Fury of Rain Storms."

The title of the poem "My fear is simple, heart-faced" comes from Lorna Dee Cervantes's poem "Love of My Flesh, Living Death."

The James Whitcomb Riley quote in "All Things Rare" comes from his poem "Out to Old Aunt Mary's."

THANKS

Much thanks and gratitude to the following people, without whom this collection would have been impossible—my professors, Angela Ball, Julia Johnson, and Tyehimba Jess; T.A. Noonan, who's probably laid some sort of healing hand on each of these pieces; Meagan Cass, Rhonda Lott, Sarah Powell, Katherine Adams, Benjamin Morris, Daniel Crocker, Josh Webster, Anthony Abboreno, Scott Fynboe, Jeffrey MacLachlin, Gary Charles Wilkens, Lindsay Walker, Wendy Derrick, Patrick Rettger, Lauren McKee, Mary Miller, Ryan Davidson, Allison Riddles, and Cherri Conley, for the love, support, and late night beer runs; William Wright, Dan Morris, Richard Boada, Jennifer Westfield, Mary Ann O'Gorman, Greg Weiss, Joanna Meadvin, Katherine Cozzens, Deja Early, Jordan Sanderson, John Wang, Eric Flynt, and everyone else at the Center for Writers for three years of workshop and mayhem.

ABOUT THE AUTHOR

Erin Elizabeth Smith is the author of *The Fear of Being Found* (Three Candles Press 2008) and *The Chainsaw Bears* (Dancing Girl Press 2010). Her poems have appeared in numerous journals, including *32 Poems, New Delta Review, Yalobusha Review, Water~Stone, Cimarron Review,* and *RHINO*. She teaches in the English Department at the University of Tennessee and serves as the managing editor of *Stirring: A Literary Collection* and the *Best of the Net Anthology*.

CPSIA information can be obtained at www.ICGtesting.com
Printed in the USA
LVOW08s0626110714

393864LV00004B/200/P

9 780982 630983